Julia Seal

The Balloon Chase

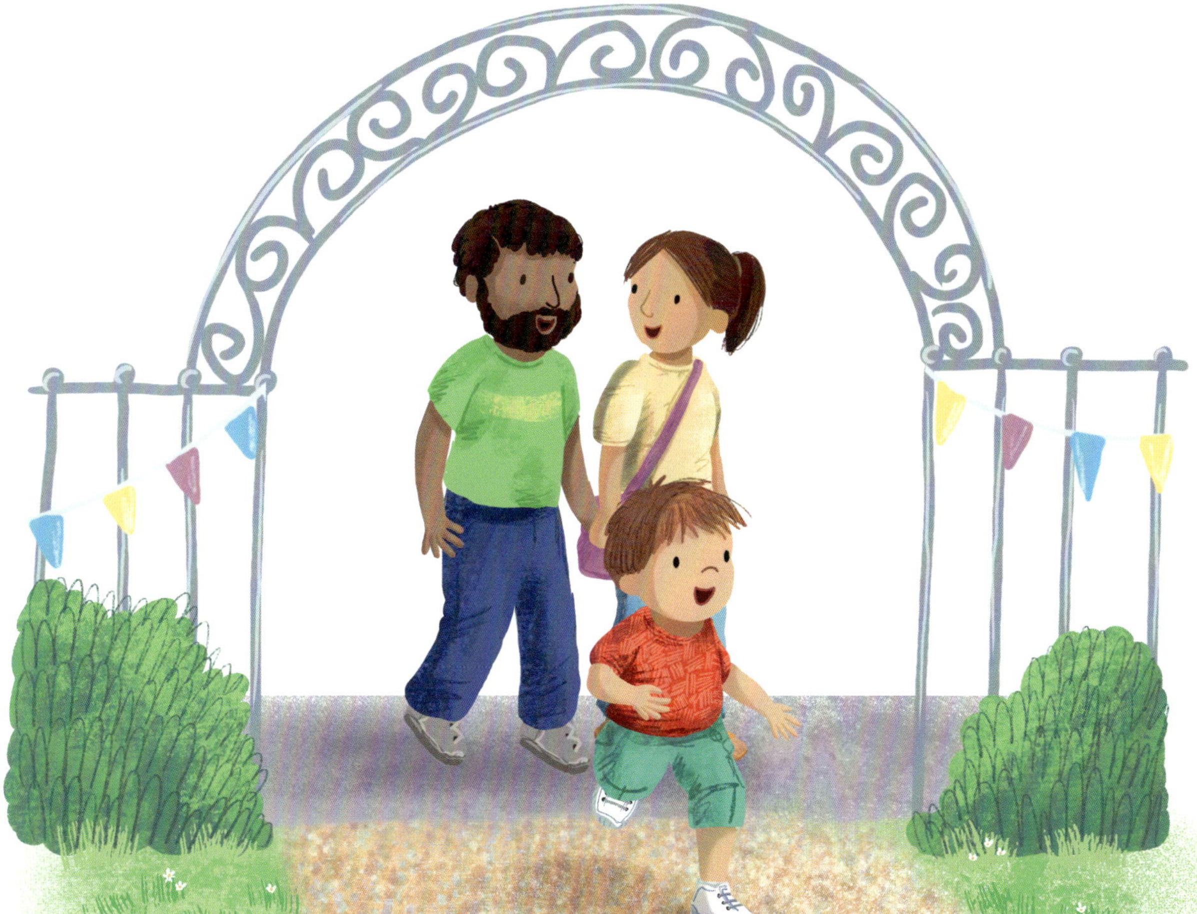

Collins

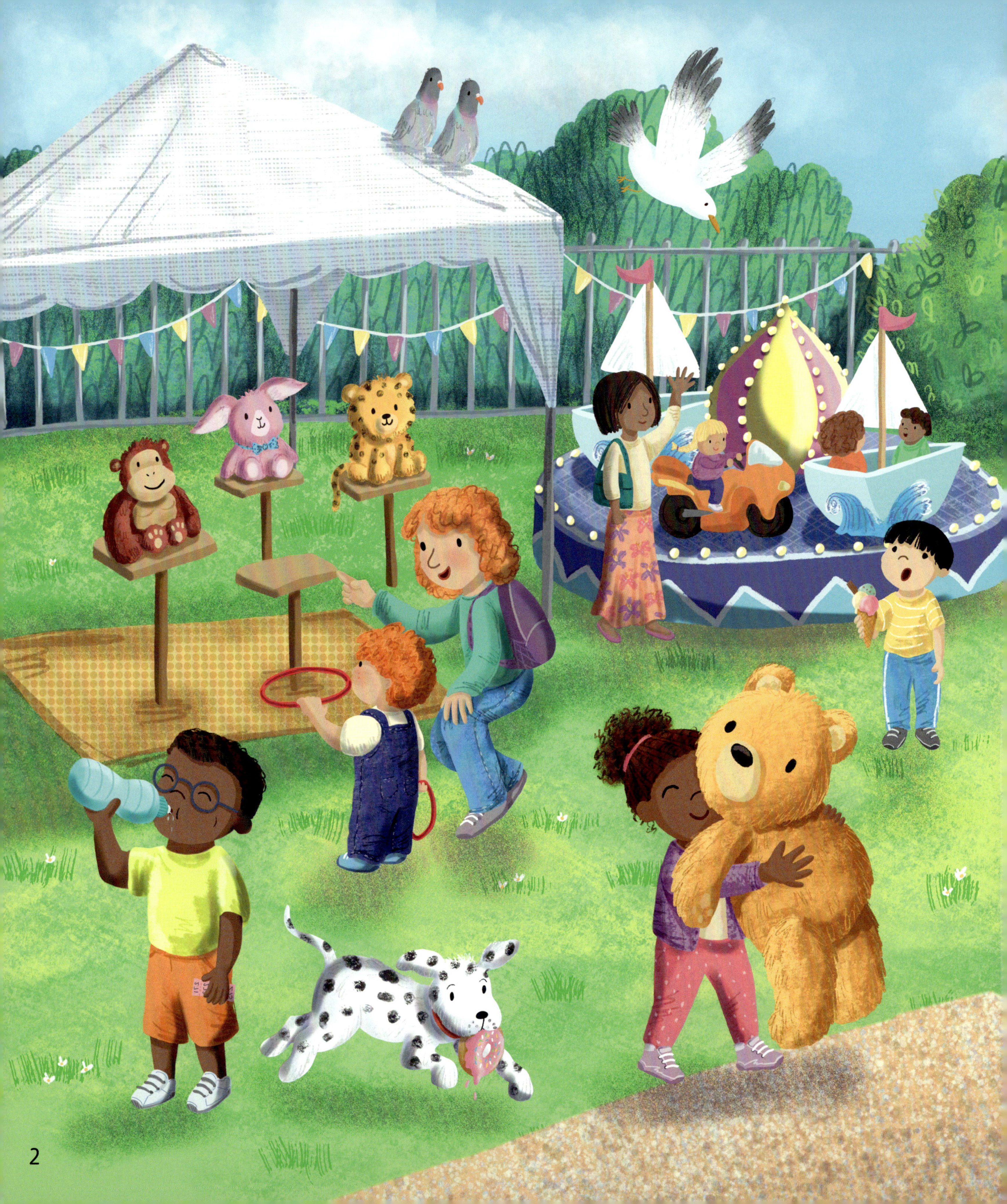

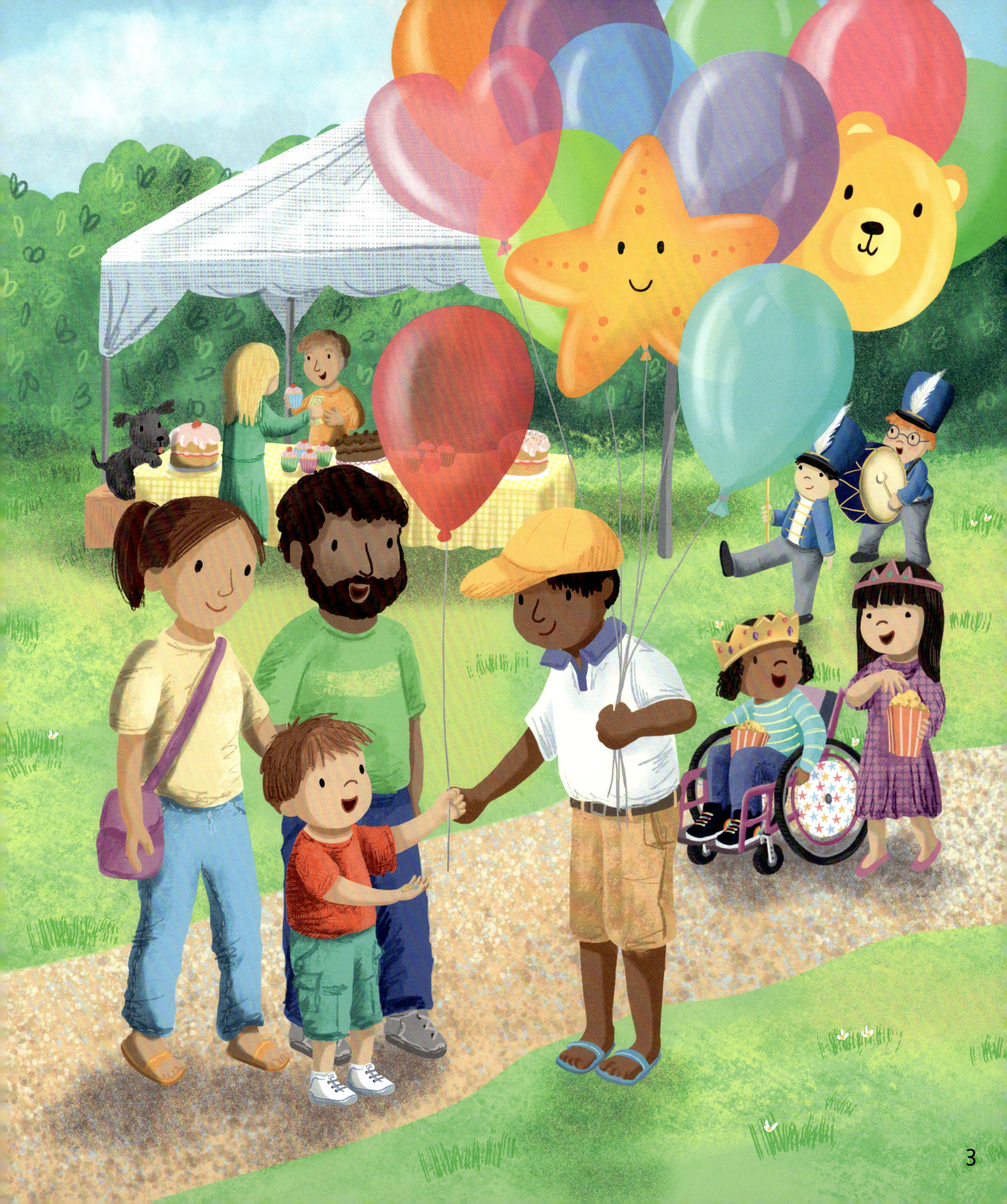

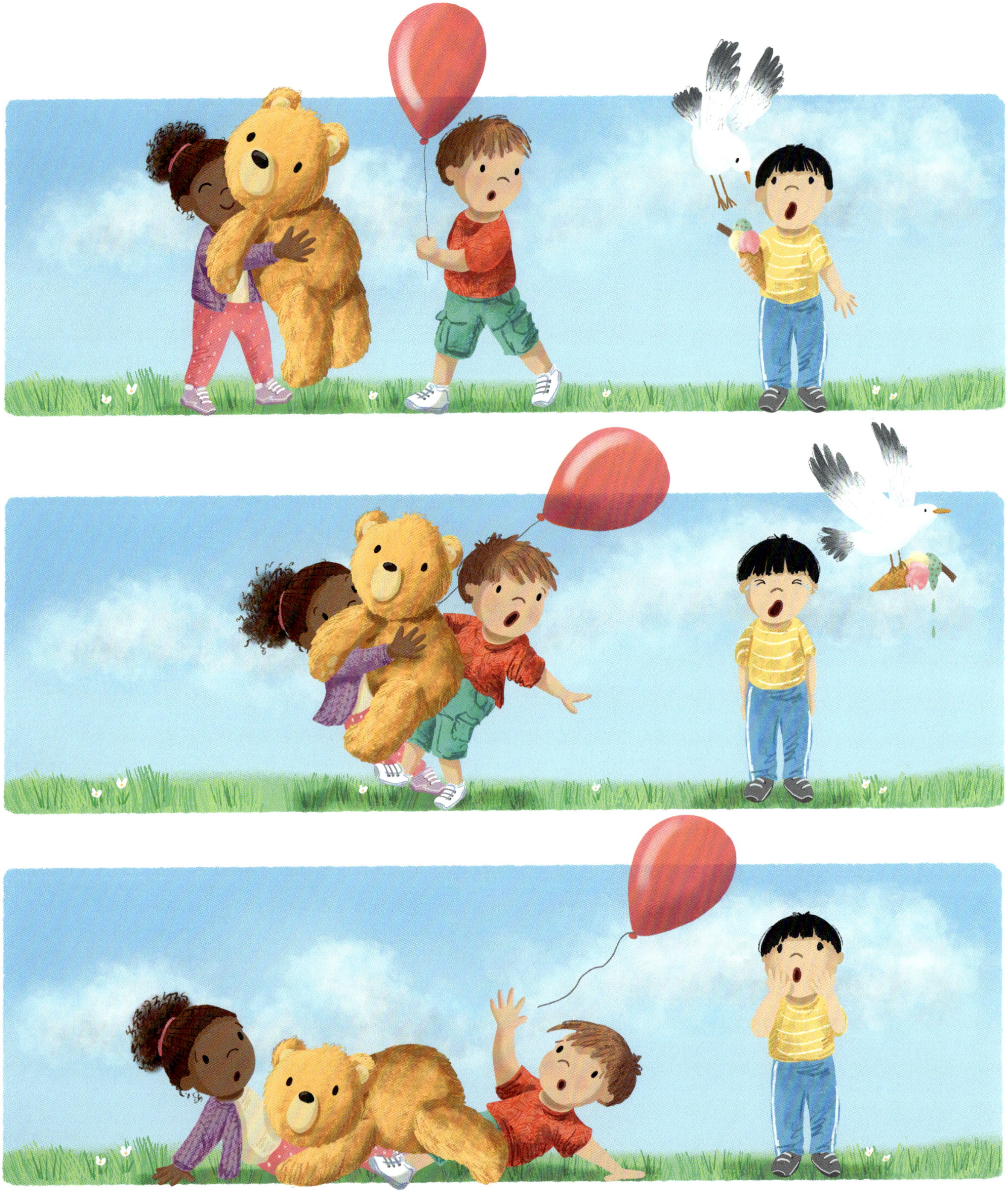

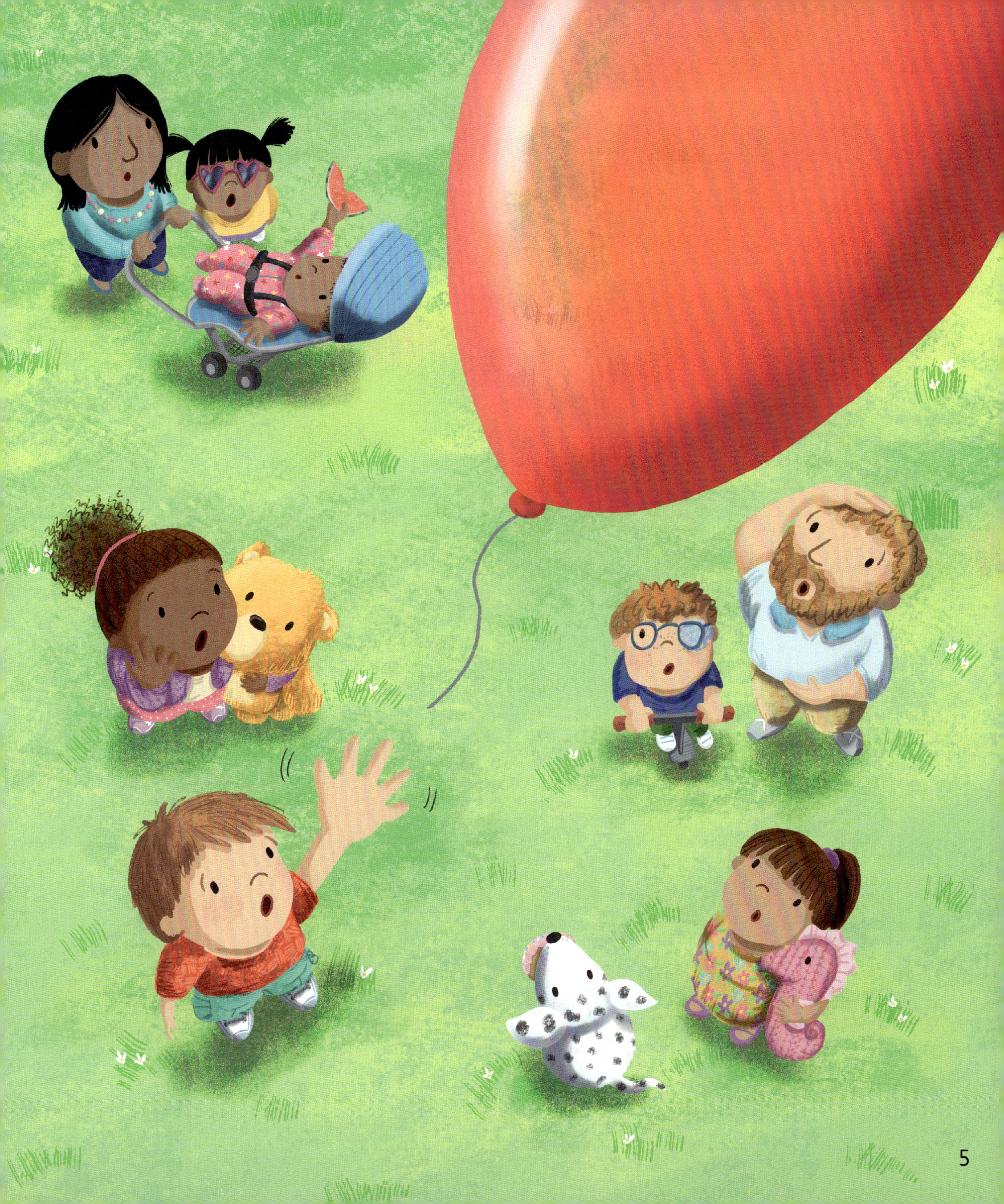

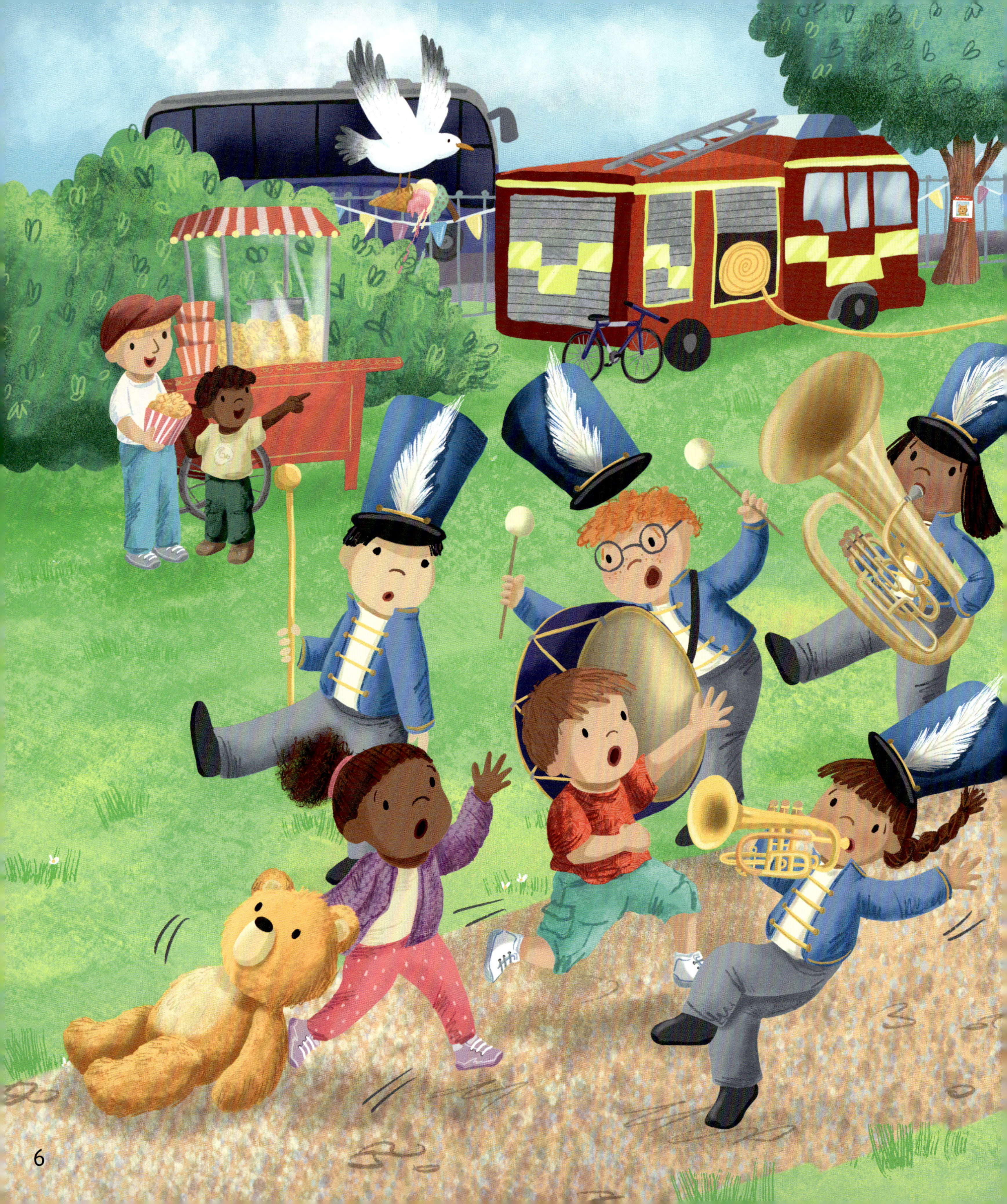

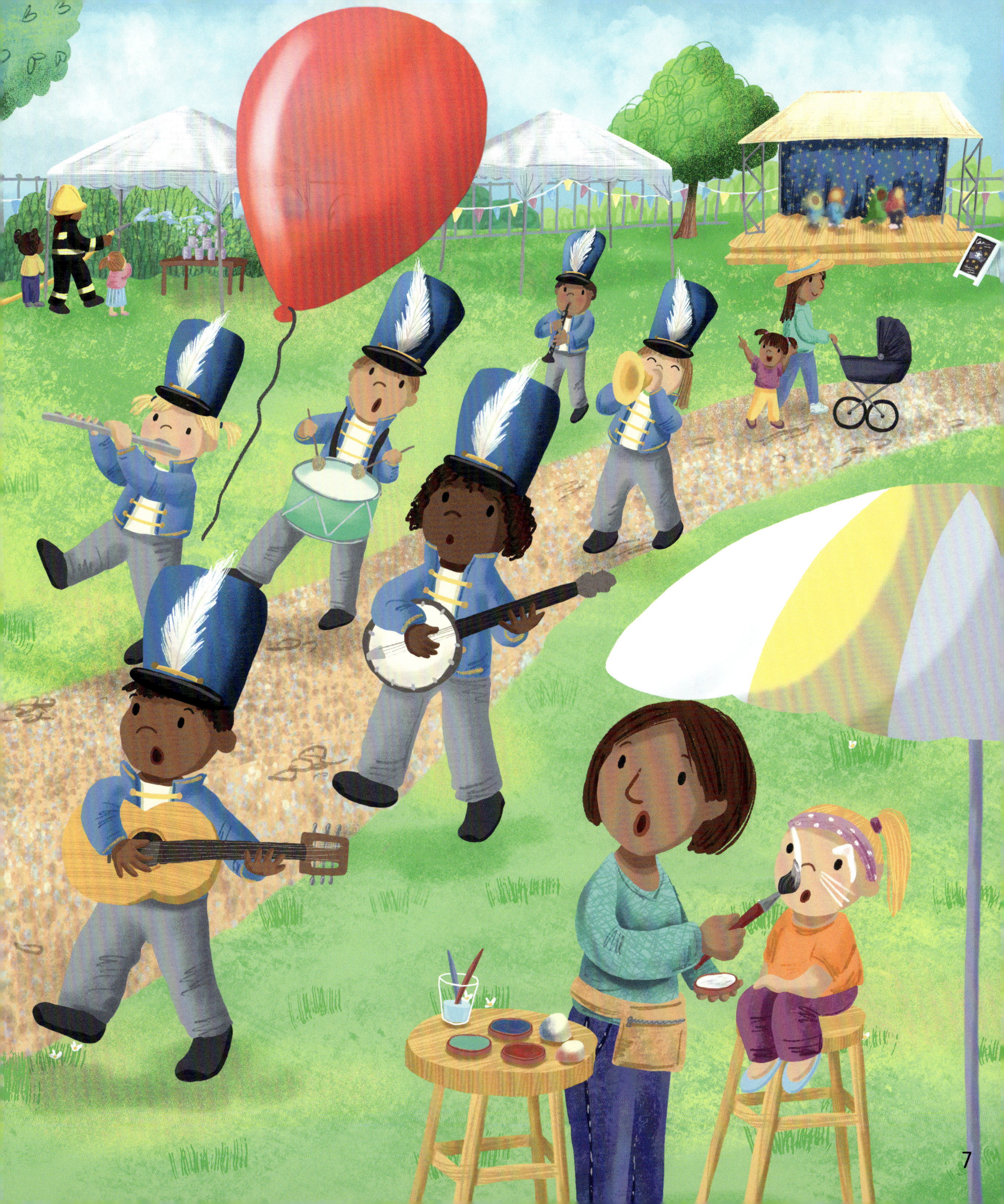

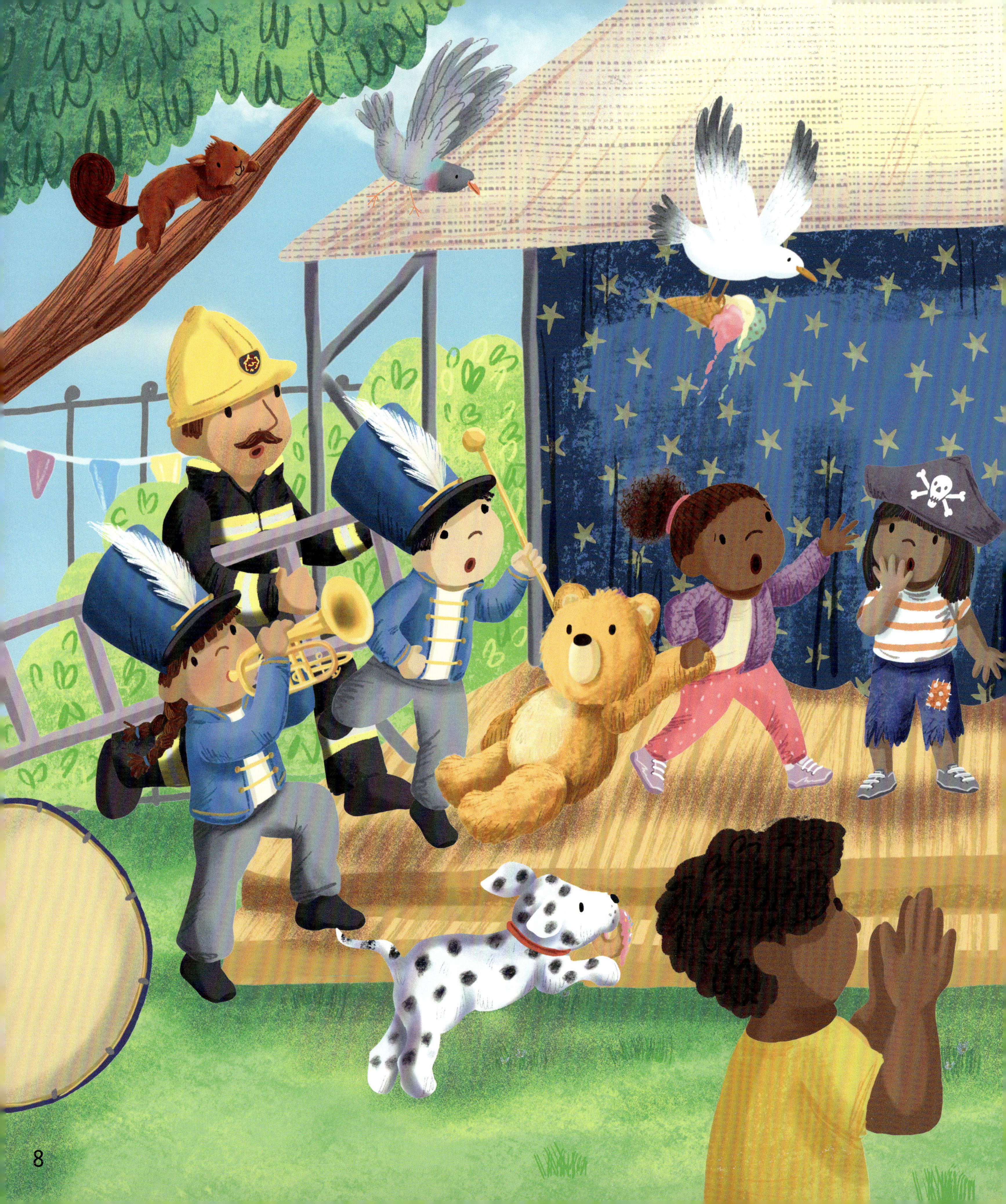

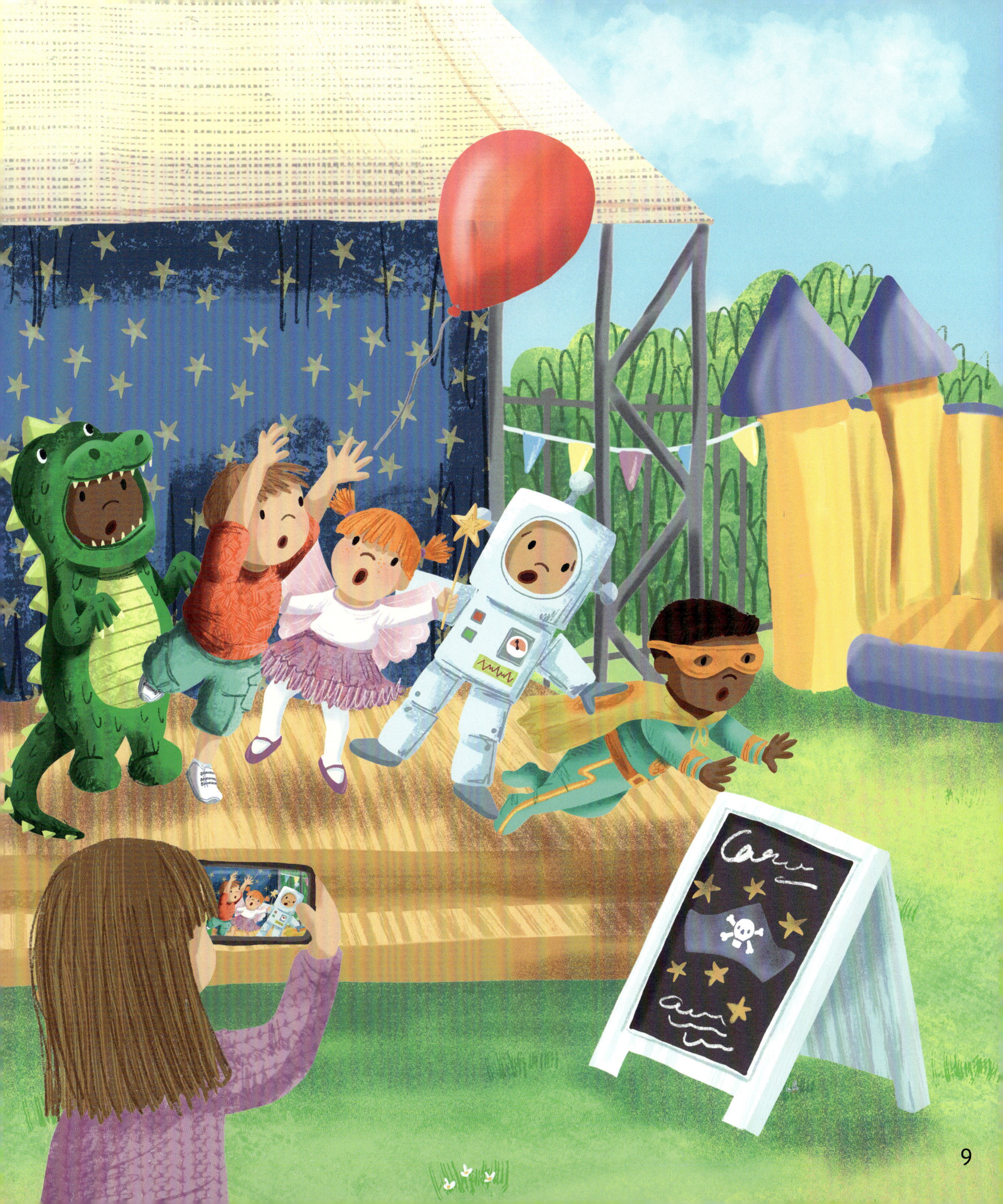

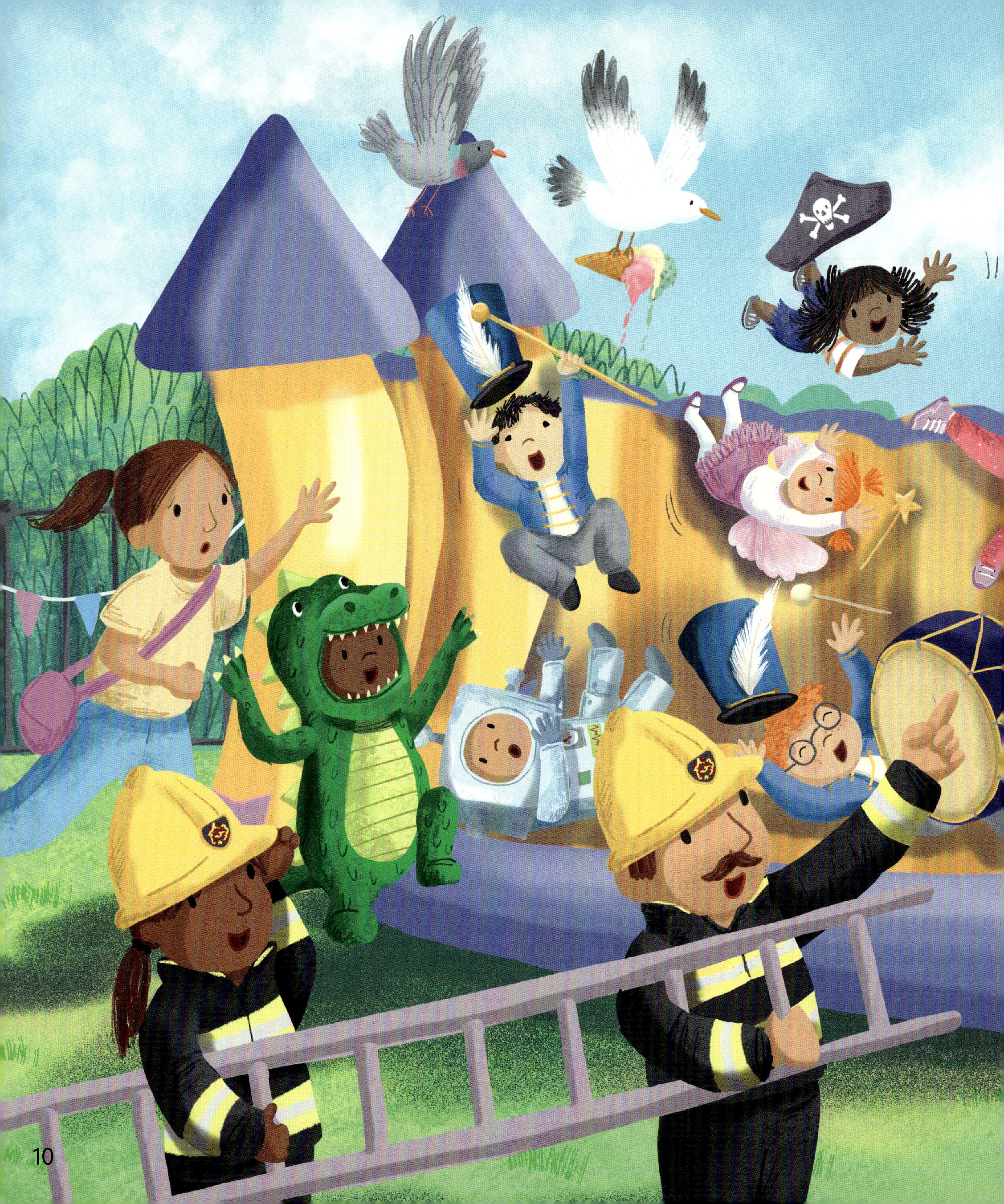

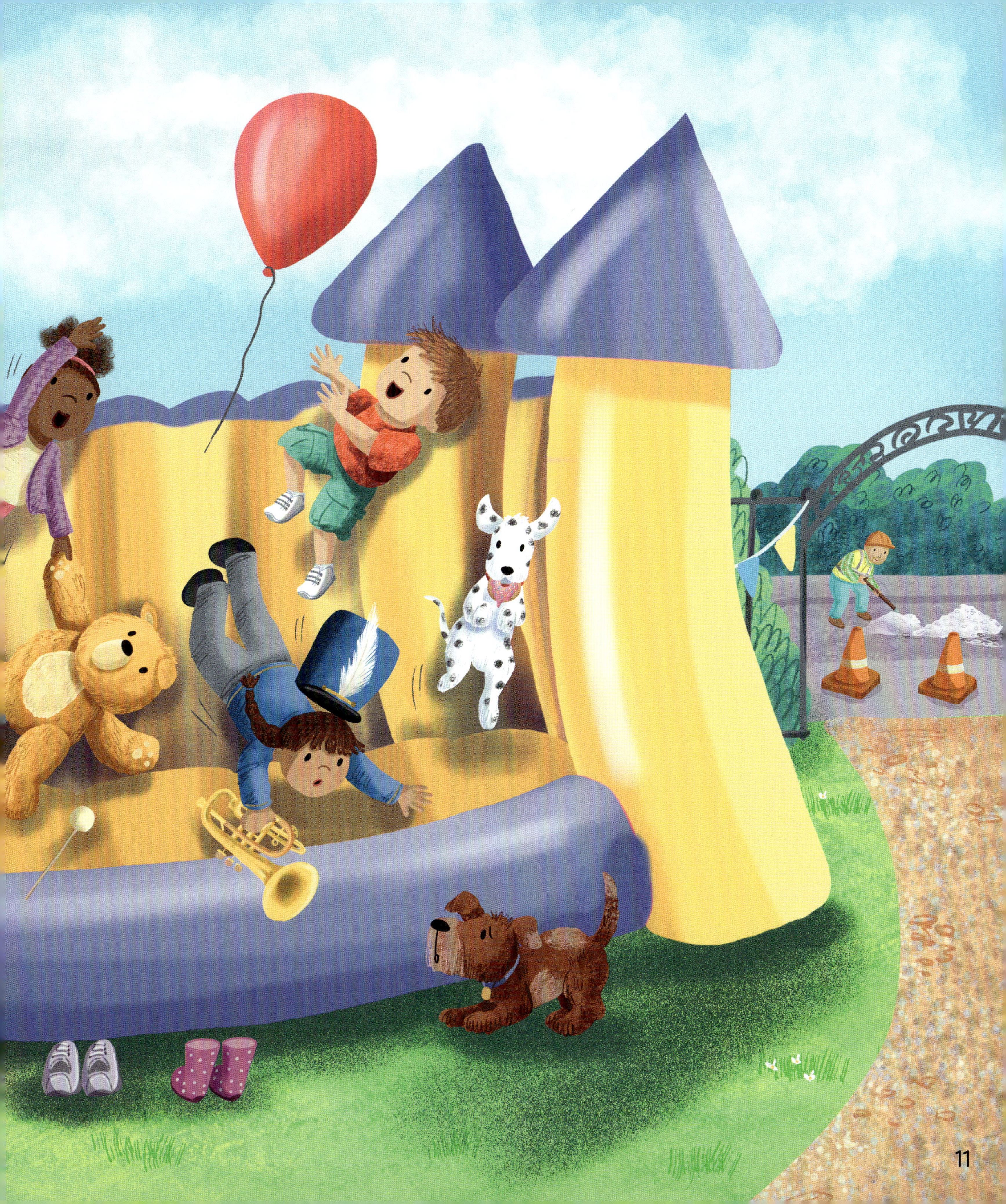

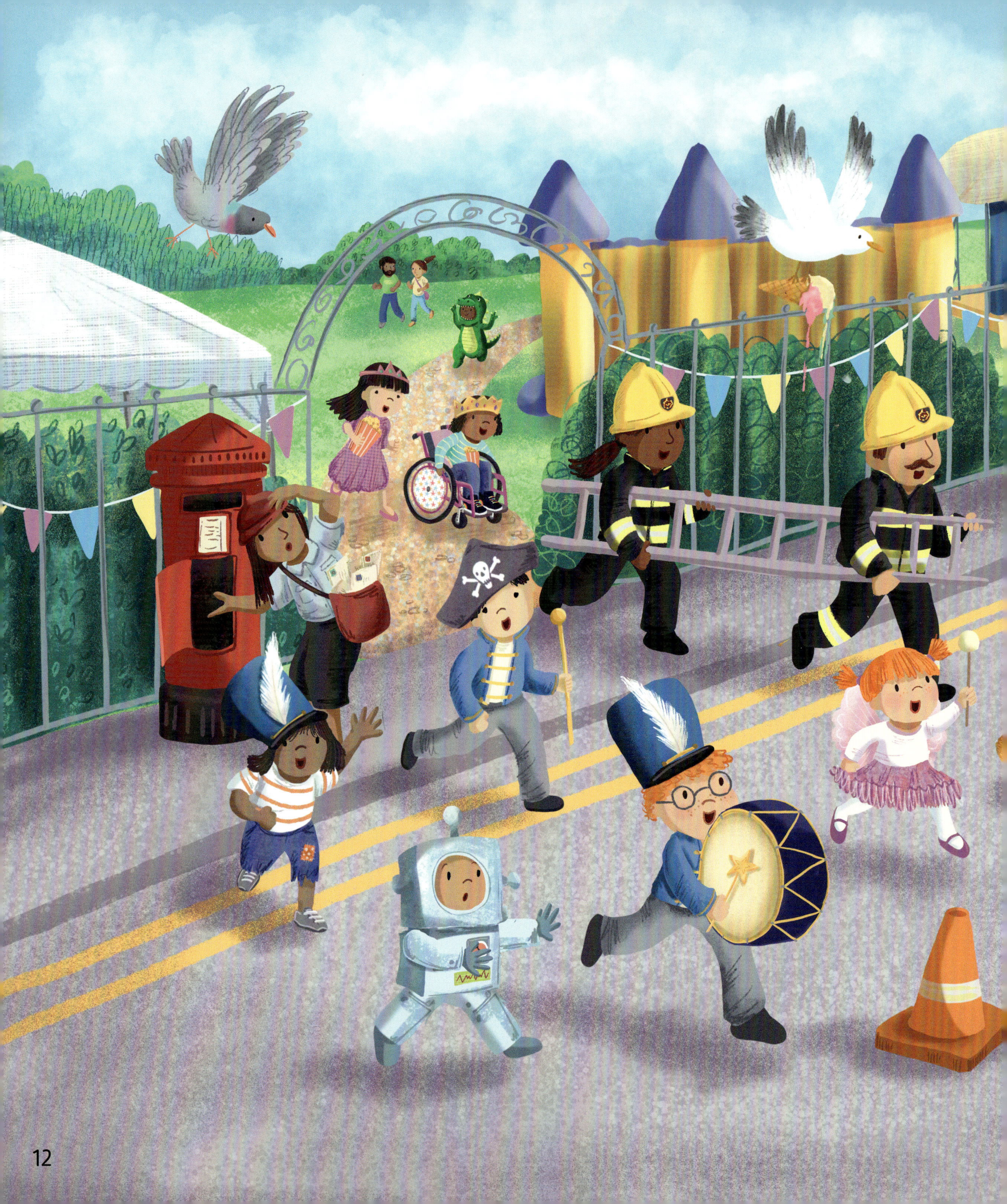

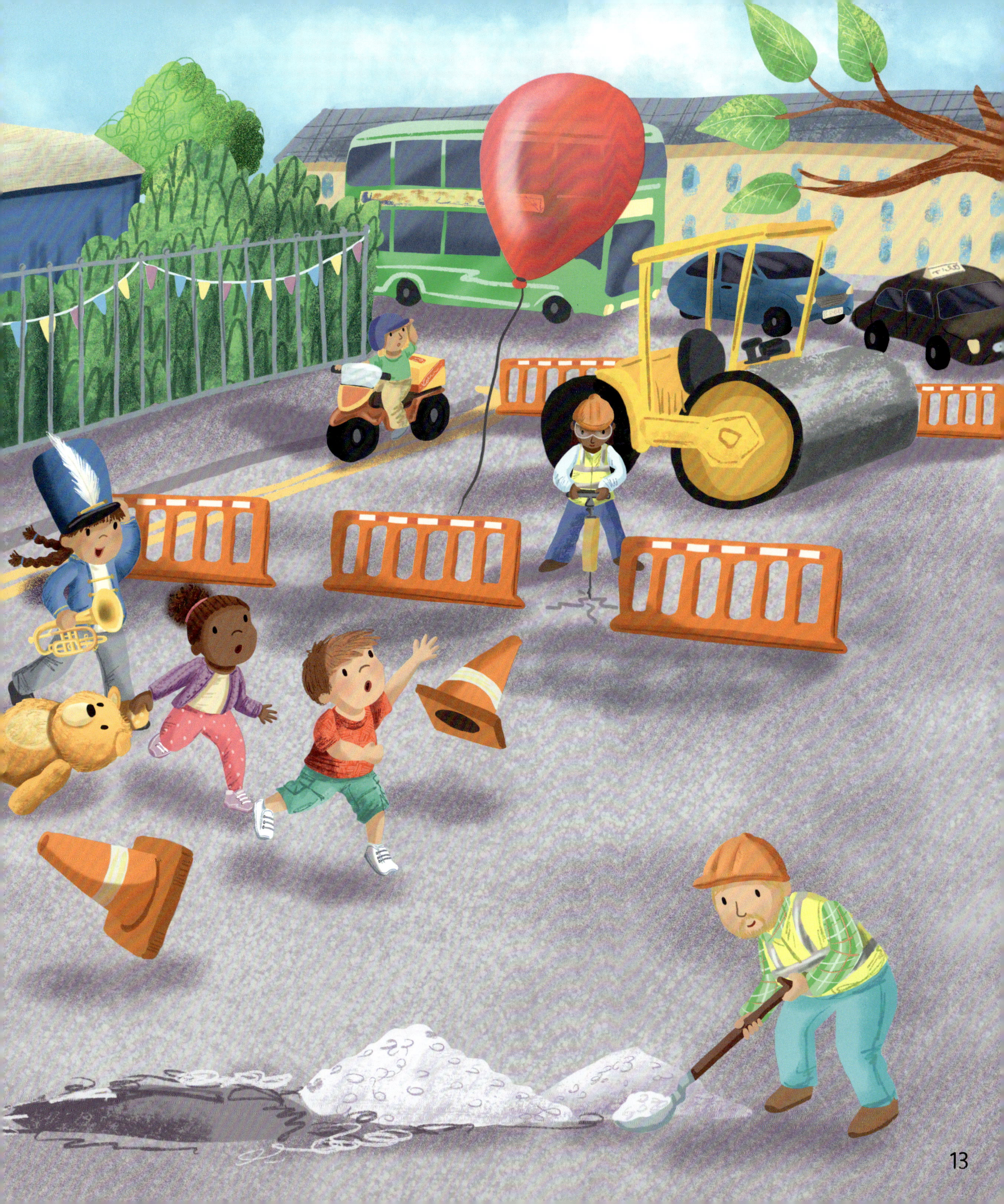

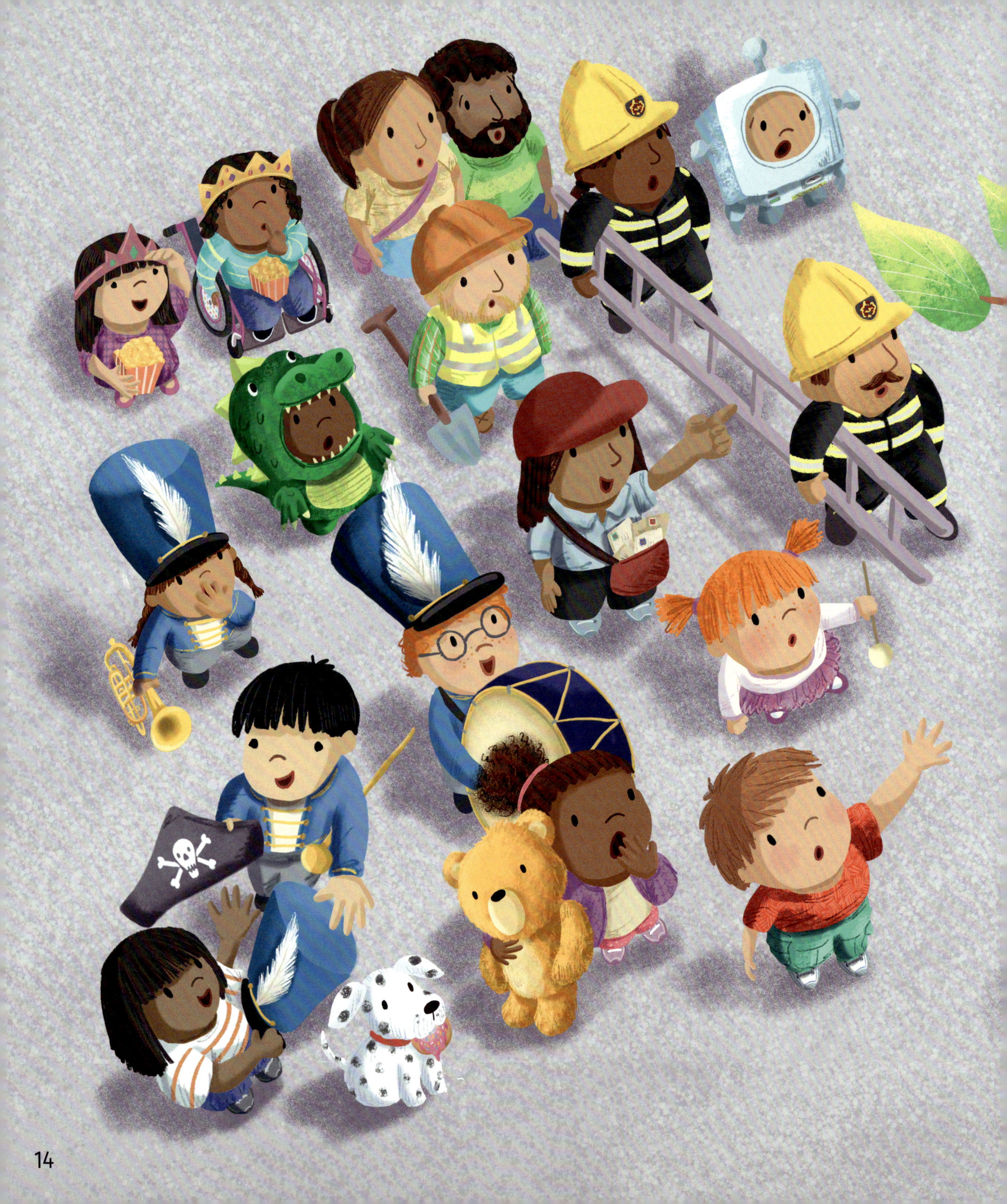

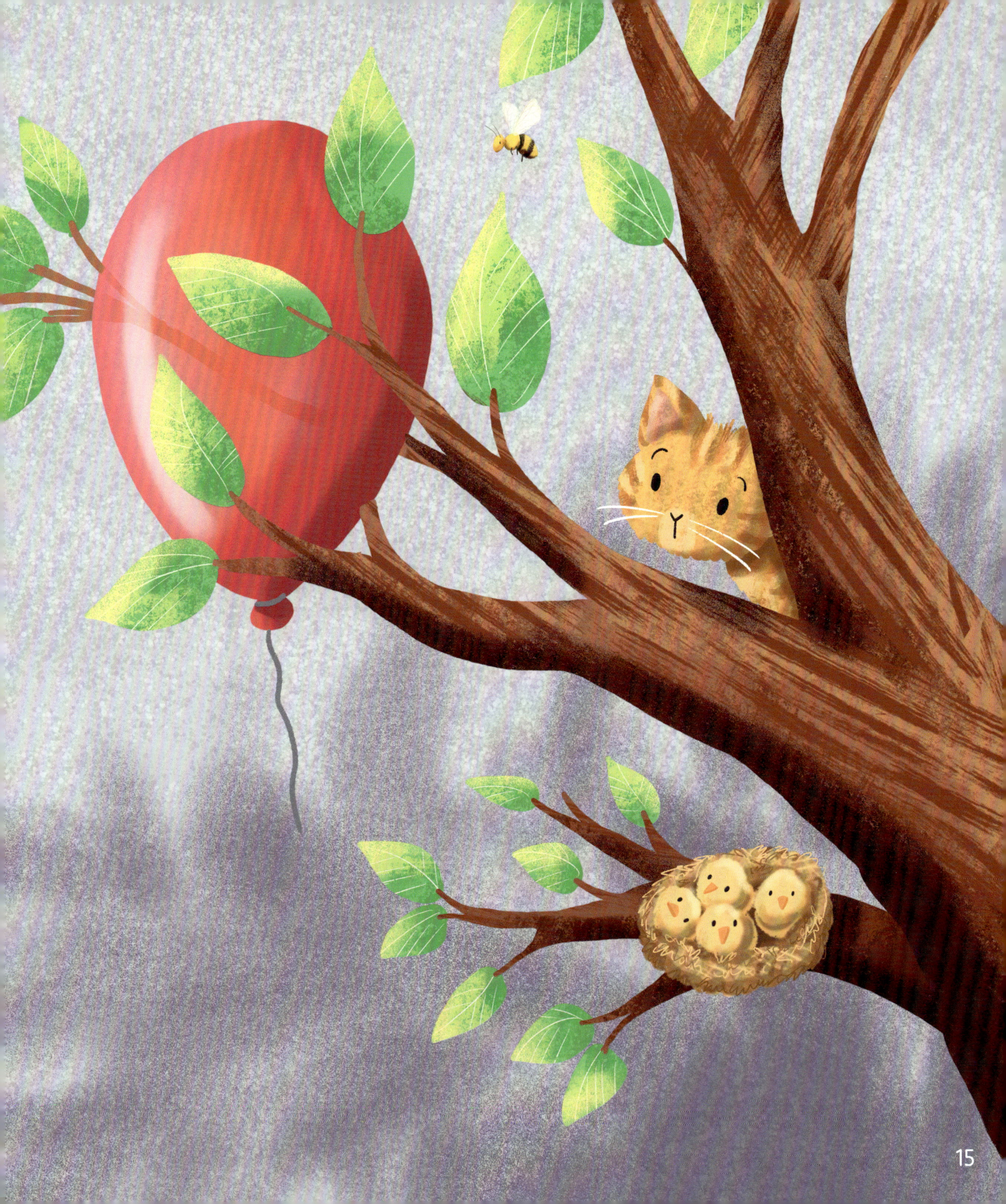

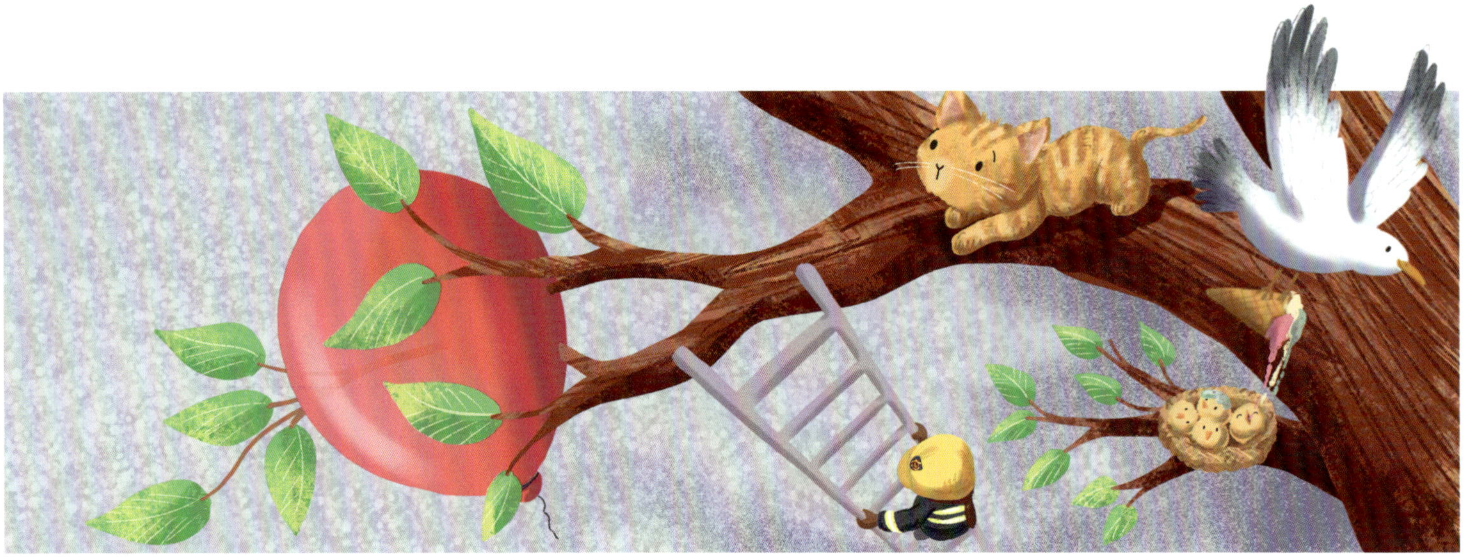

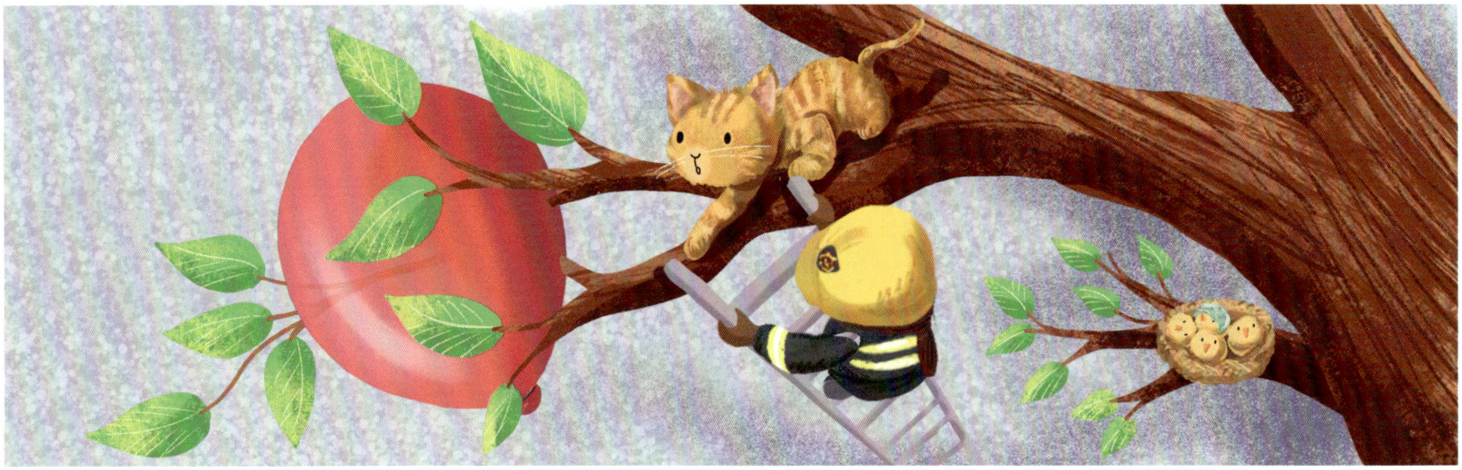

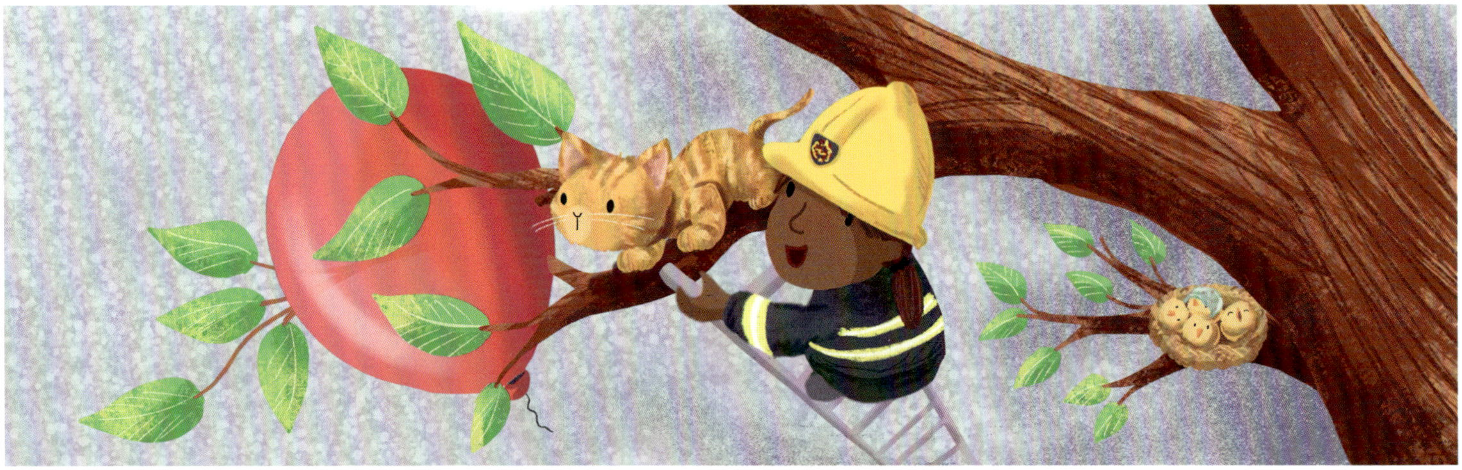

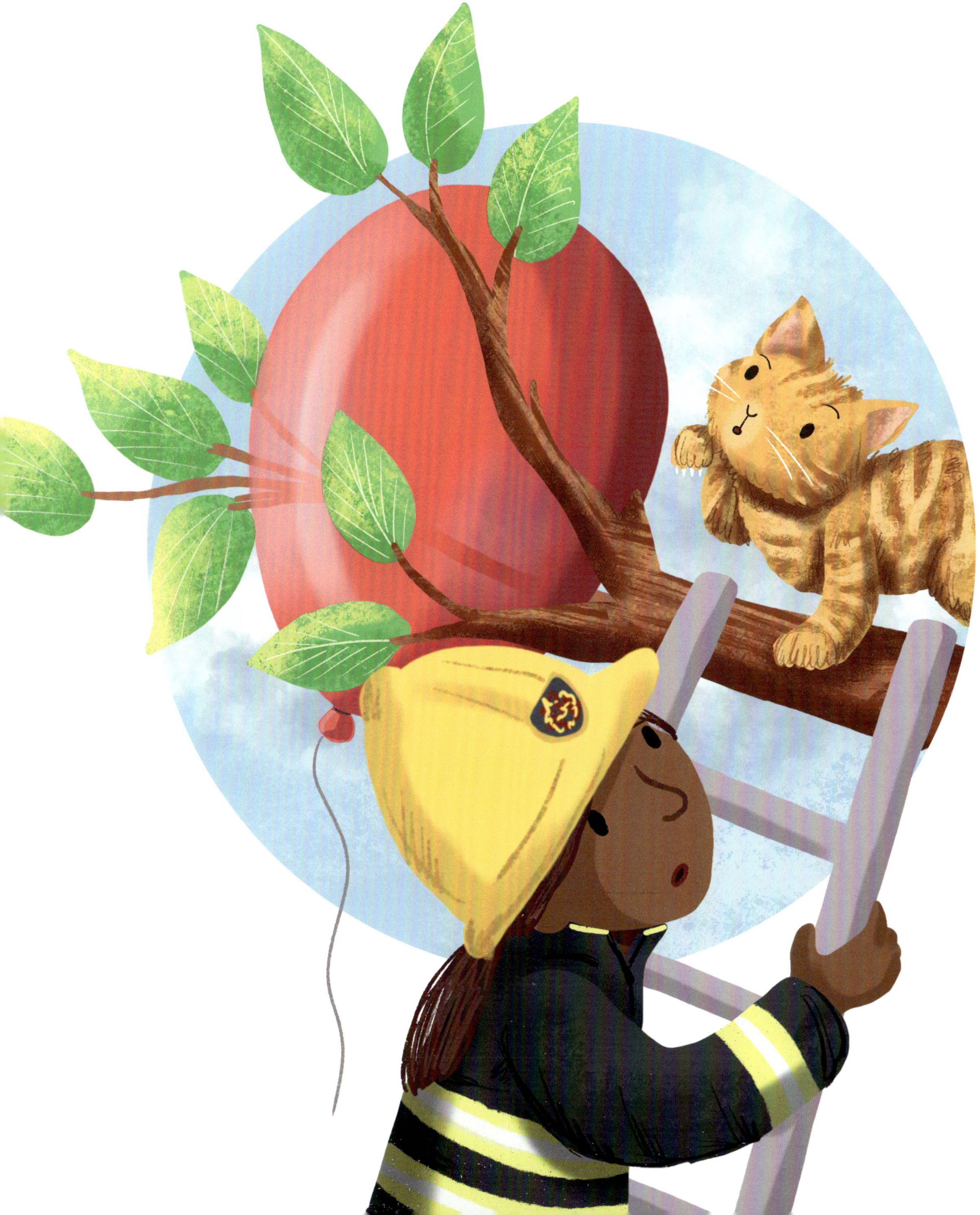

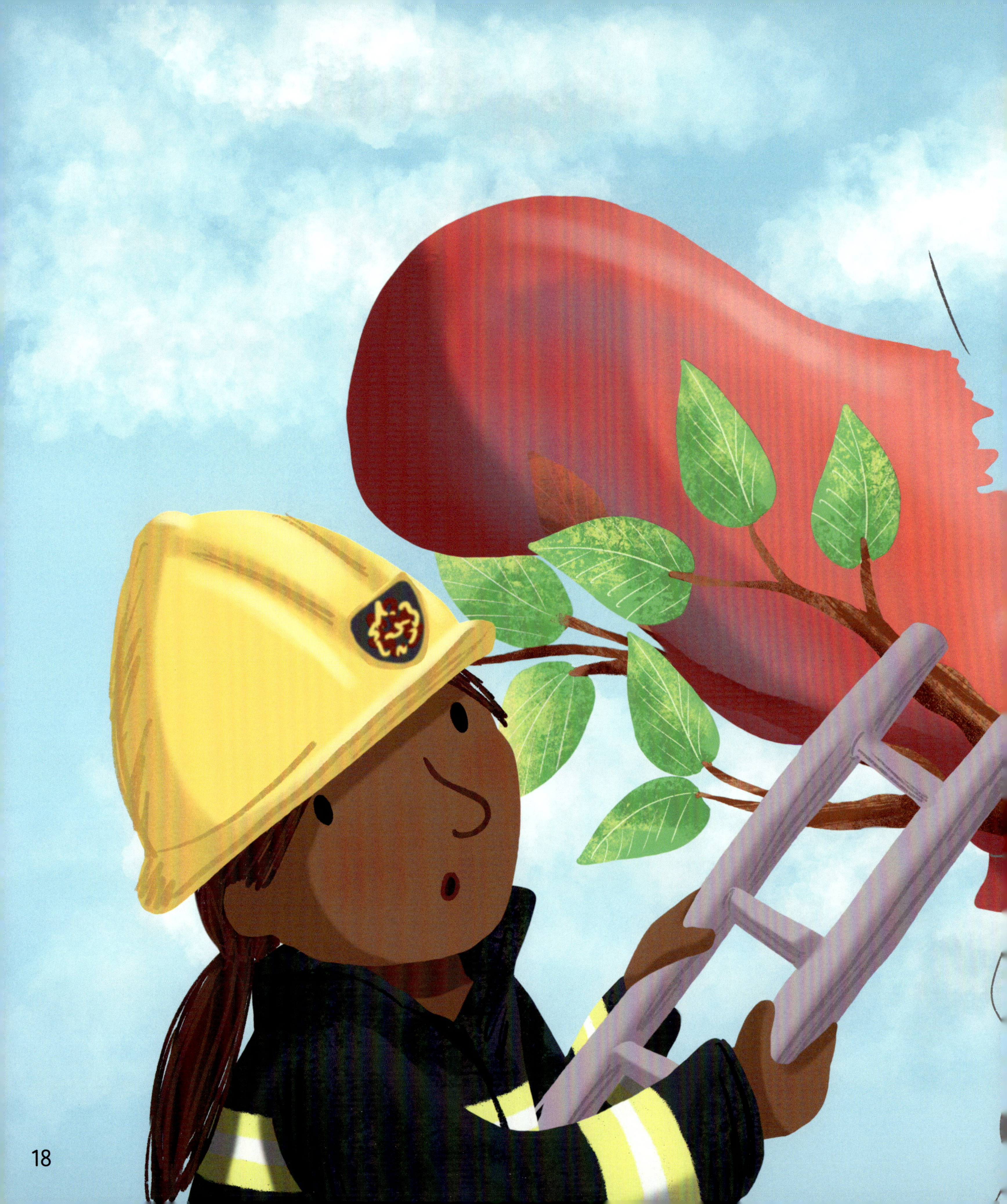

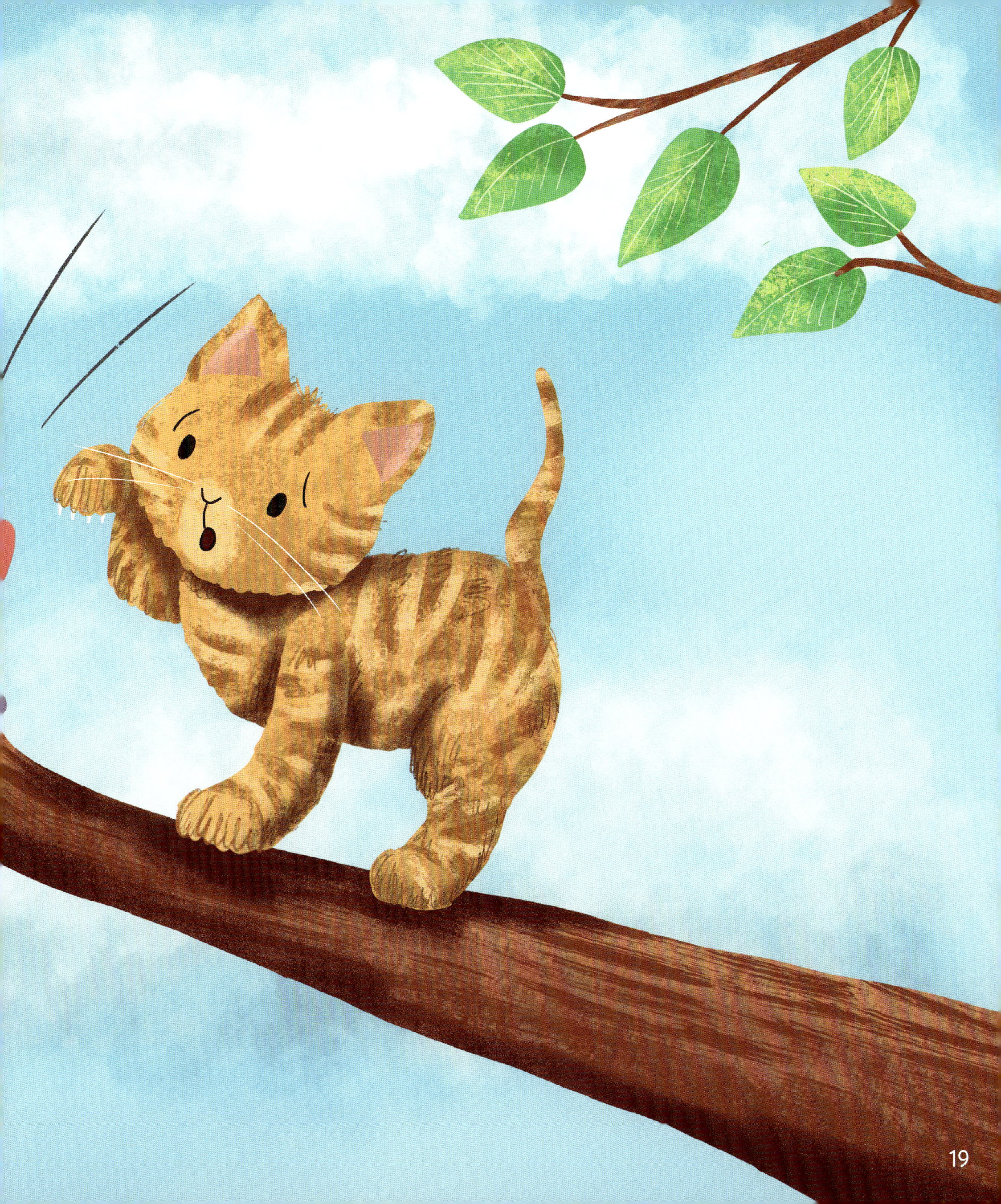

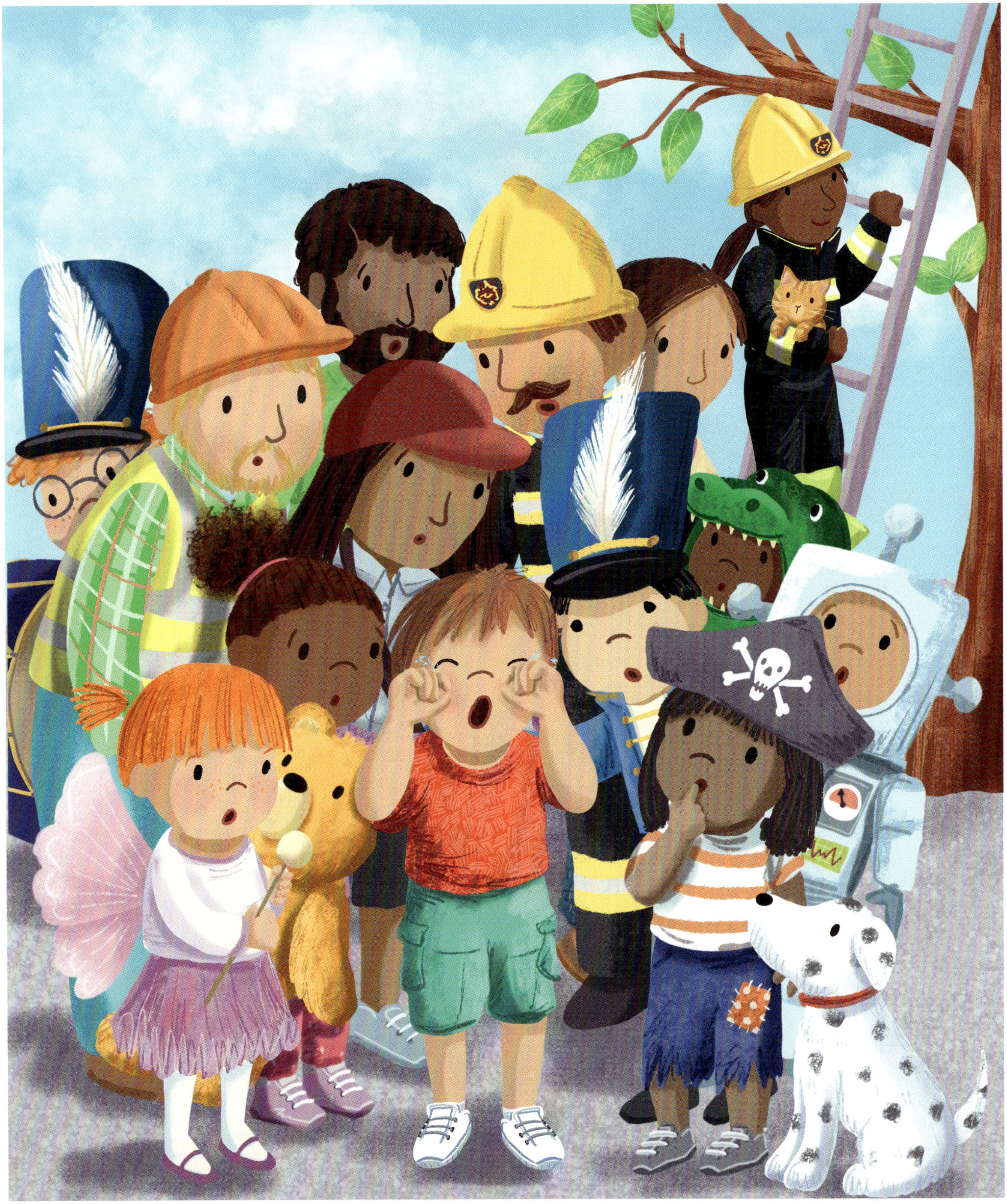

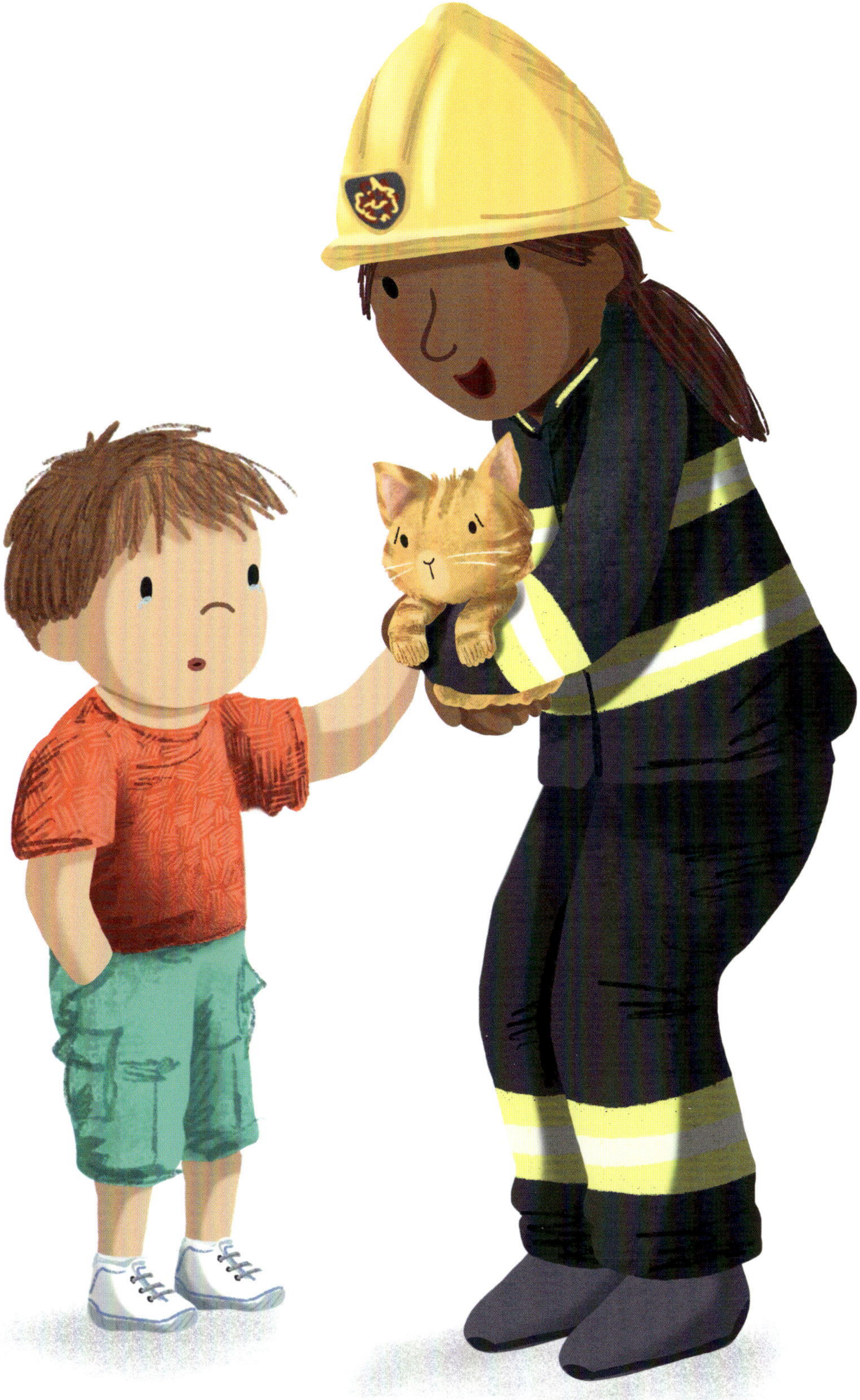

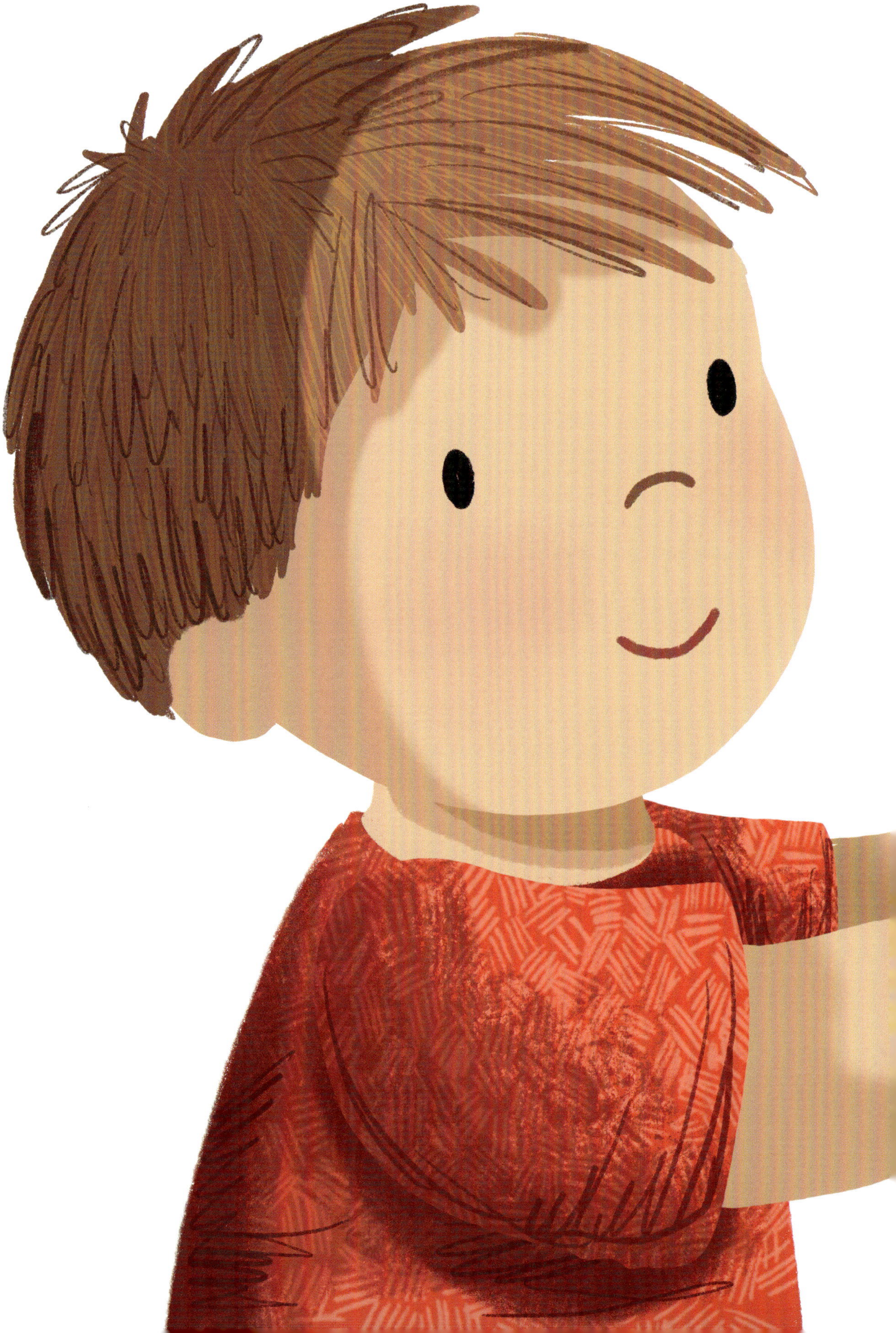

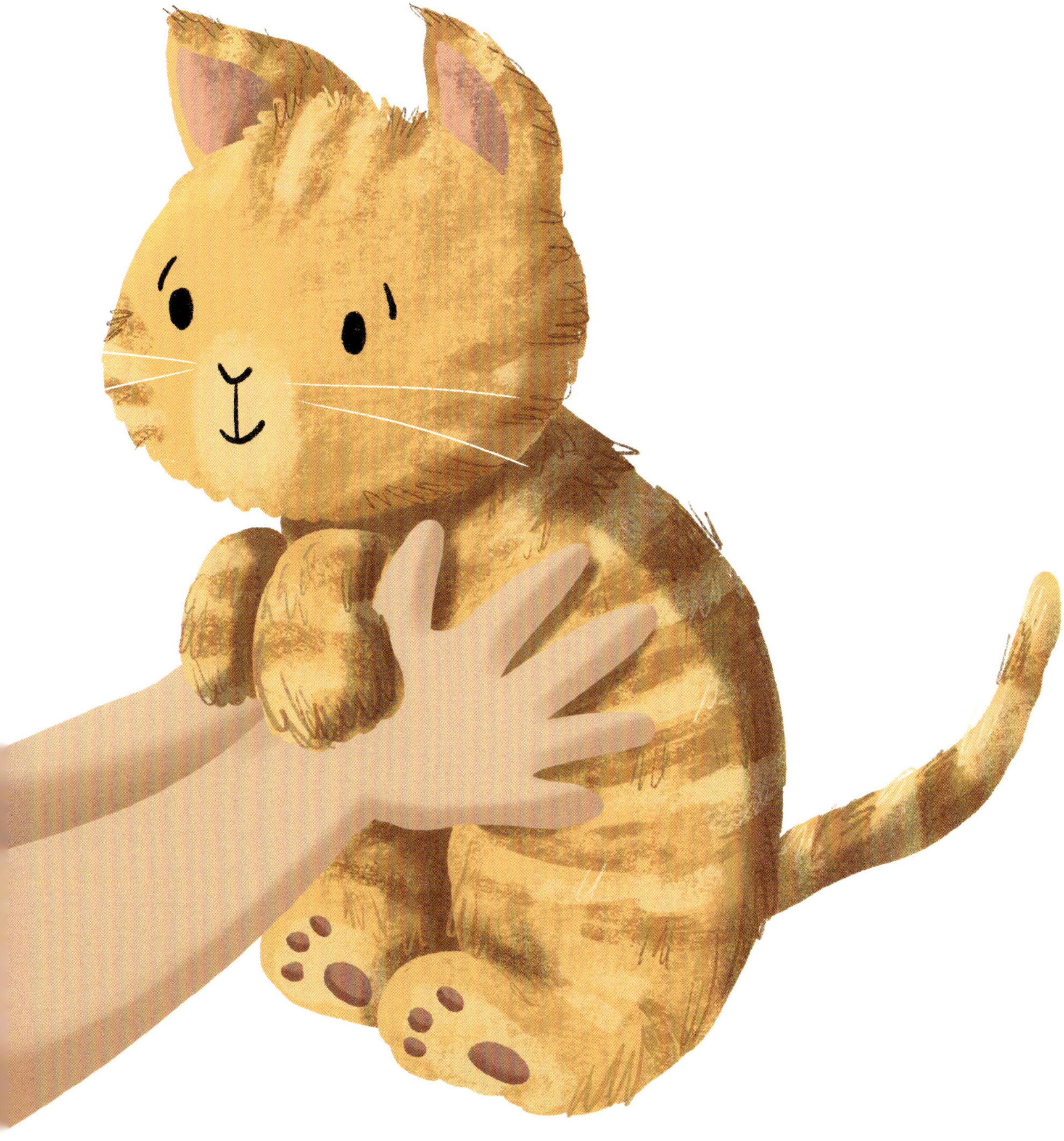

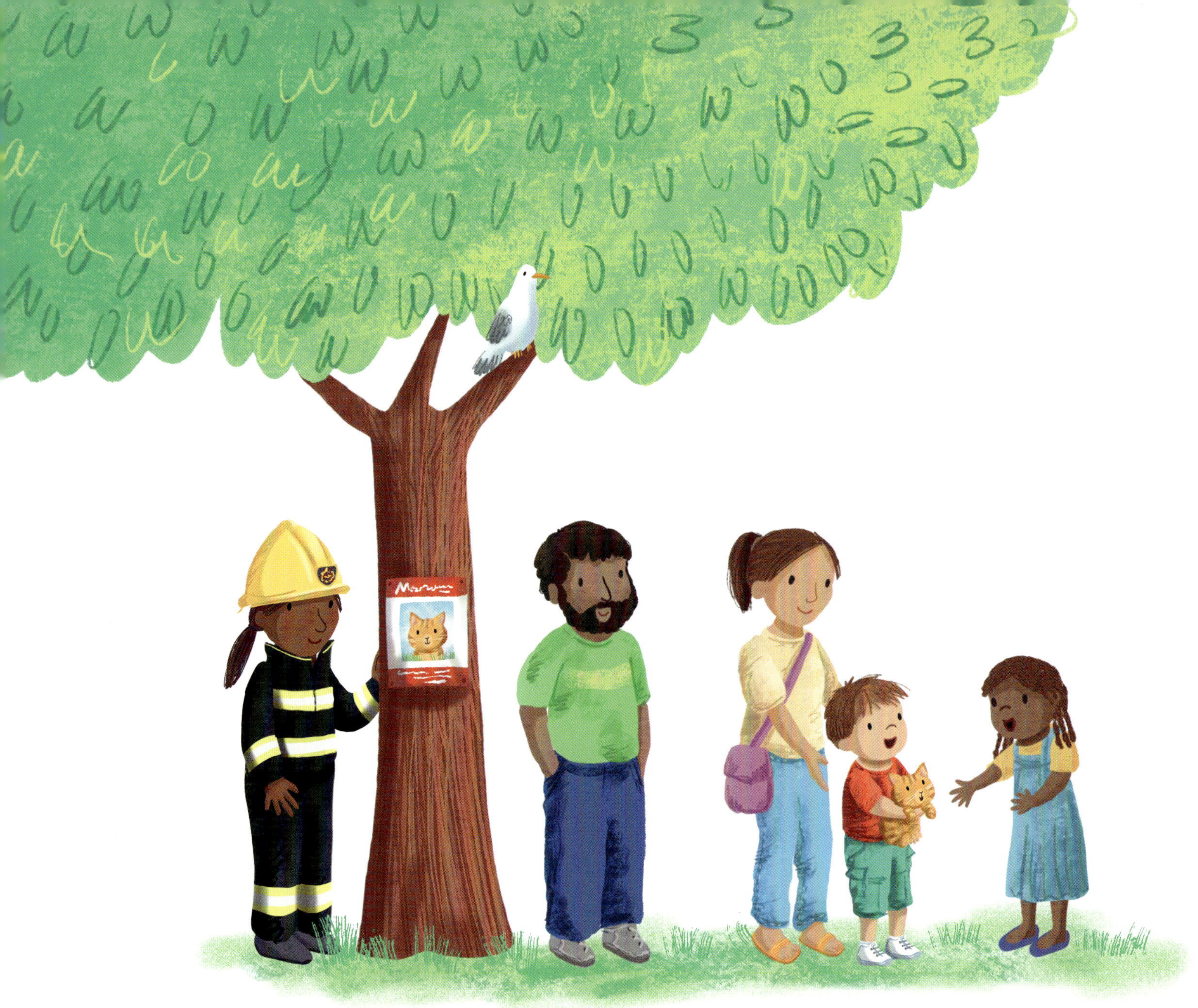